The Deal

My Little Book of Grief

Ernest Vasey

MAPLE
PUBLISHERS

The Deal - My Little Book of Grief

Author: Ernest Vasey

Copyright © Ernest Vasey (2024)

The right of Ernest Vasey to be identified as author of this work has been asserted by the author in accordance with section 77 and 78 of the Copyright, Designs and Patents Act 1988.

First Published in 2024

ISBN 978-1-83538-003-1 (Paperback)
     978-1-83538-004-8 (Ebook)

Cover Design and Book Layout by:
     White Magic Studios
     www.whitemagicstudios.co.uk

Cover picture, Cheryl Vasey her lAS school photo

Published by:
     Maple Publishers
     Fairbourne Drive, Atterbury,
     Milton Keynes,
     MK10 9RG, UK
     www.maplepublishers.com

A CIP catalogue record for this title is available from the British Library.

All rights reserved. No part of this book may be reproduced or translated by any form or by any means, electronic or mechanical, including photocopying, recording or by any information storage and retrieval system without written permission from the author.

The views expressed in this work are solely those of the author and do not necessarily reflect the views of the publisher, and the publisher hereby disclaims any responsibility for them.

Introduction

Welcome to my little book of grief. This book has been incredibly difficult to write from an emotional and personal perspective, as it follows my own journey from normal everyday life, to being tragically thrown into my own grieving process. I would like this book to be in memory of my daughter Cheryl Vasey whose loss changed the course of my life forever. For the reader I would like the book to be an insightful journey through one person's grieving process. The book is intentionally small in the hope it may help those currently grieving to have a bite size real life perspective of grief. The book is not aimed solely at those who are grieving but for those who may want to be better positioned to help those who are grieving, or simply to read a real life journey through grief and the feelings encountered through a shattering loss. With the benefit of hindsight and education I will highlight where I was in my grieving process (Grief, Denial, Anger, Bargaining, Depression, and finally Acceptance) throughout my story.

I say hindsight and education as I was thrust into unimaginable grief 24 years ago, and education because over the past 24 years I have become a psychotherapist and founder/CEO of one of the largest homeless charities in the North East of England, both have proved to be emotionally challenging and also rewarding. I would hope my therapeutic experience of grief, coupled with my real life story will make things a little more understandable for those that find themselves in a similar situation to me, or have a desire to learn more.

Before I start my story, it may be helpful to look at what grief is. I believe that grief underpins almost everything that a client presents to a therapist. It always goes back to the loss of something that has brought them to the therapist's office. Whether it be loss of an individual, loss or break up of a relationship, loss of self esteem or resilience, almost everything relates back to the grieving process that we will cover together in this little book of grief. This generalization may not make me popular in the therapeutic community, perhaps its just my simplistic view in what has gradually become an overcrowded and intellectualized profession. Understanding grief is best explained in its simplest form, I find jargon and intellectualizing topics really confusing for someone in the grip of trauma, so from this point forward simplicity is the key.

When asked to describe the grieving process I usually use the easiest and most widely known process that we have all experienced at some point in our lives, losing a set of keys!

The loss of keys could easily be transferred to mobile phone or something similar. Imagine an everyday item that is significant to you and is very impactful when misplaced. For the benefit of this example, I will use keys.

We have all been in that situation when we are about to leave home and reach for our keys but they're not where we would have expected them to be. Almost immediately the first stage of the grieving process kicks in, **denial**. We will experience feelings of confusion, fear or shock. We leave the place where we know the keys ought to be only to return periodically during the search because that is where they should be. We are simply denying the fact that they are not there. We then move into the **anger** stage. Feelings of anger irritation and anxiety may be prevalent. The anger may be aimed at ourselves for being 'so stupid to lose them' or at someone else who must have moved them. We then enter the **bargaining** phase 'ok if I can just find these keys, I will ensure

I always put them in a safe place'. Then **depression** sets in as we realise, we are likely to be late for the appointment you were about to leave home for, and experience feelings of hopelessness that may feel overwhelming. Eventually we will enter the **acceptance** phase, where we accept the world where the keys no longer exist, and we start to look at our options. In this phase we may start making phone calls or making alternative arrangements because we are accepting that life needs to go on without the keys. This is a very simplistic overview of the grieving process, acceptance of the world where the significant thing or person no longer exists is our long term goal.

I have picked out in *italics* relevant stages of my own journey through the grieving process while relaying my story to allow you the reader an insight into grief from the safety of my experience. The reader may see themselves through my journey and gain some understanding of the feelings they are experiencing.

Hi, my name's Ernest Stephen Vasey and I'm a member of an exclusive club that nobody wants to be a member of, I'm a grieving parent.

As I reread the following account of my daughter's death and the weeks and months afterward some 24 years later, I have been gripped with fear as to what I may remember that had been buried over time, or the emotions it may raise that I had long since learned to live with and control.

I have been fearful and felt physically sick. I have thought of how life can deal you 24 hours of complete opposites that test every single sinew of your whole being. I have lived for 59 years and yet a split-second lapse of someone's concentration has changed the lives of so many people. I have skipped these sections so many times during the edit because I find them too painful to read. When I start reading the accident section it's like opening a dark heavy door into an empty room then closing it behind me. The door can't be left ajar to allow a sense of escape or to allow light in, when you're in, you're in. There is no half measure, you must totally commit to the situation. What's scary is not knowing whether I will be the same person exiting the room as I was entering, that's how powerful and emotive grief is.

Here is the story of the day I became a grieving parent. It was coming to the end of the six weeks school summer holidays on Saturday, 30th August 1997. My teenage daughter Cheryl had spent much of her holiday watching re-runs of Elvis Presley films. She found it strange that he always seemed to end up in fights but always got the girl. We had decided on the morning that rather than waste a lovely day we would have a trip across to the Lake District from our home in County Durham. It was a beautiful morning, which reflected how life felt in general.

I ran a small plumbing and heating business, my wife Lynn worked in a local supermarket. Both Cheryl and her elder brother Lee enjoyed good health, had friends, and had lots of interests. I think it would be fair to say we felt fortunate to be in our situation. Lee had decided he had things he wanted to do at home, and being 16 and working with me every day, I understood his need to do his own thing.

We had decided to take the scenic A66 across the North Yorkshire moorland into Cumbria. In the winter, the route is often closed down with snow barriers such is its exposed location, however in the summer months the views are outstanding. Our first point of call was Kendal. I had worked in Kendal a year or so previous and decided I would like to revisit and show Lynn and Cheryl what I know of the town. Cheryl was clearly going through something of a retro phase as she tried to get me to buy her a Jackson Five CD from Woolworths. She had little interest in Michael Jackson as a solo artist but enjoyed listening to his early work with his brothers. She also liked the younger sons of three of the Jackson Five who had formed their own band. After Kendal, we moved on to Keswick. Cheryl had a mischievous sense of humor and adventure, I am in many ways partly responsible for this and played no part in curtailing this streak she had.

On arriving in Keswick we made our way to a pub in the town centre for a bite to eat, Cheryl and I got Cumberland sausage which was a curly sausage held together inside a large Yorkshire pudding then covered in gravy. I recall Cheryl thinking the sausage tasted spicy which didn't seem to curb her appetite and soon all our plates were empty. After a walk around town we decided we had best make our way back across the Pennines to home. The journey home and through Barnard Castle again didn't disappoint with the scenery being stunning. Sadly, the views were only enjoyed by me as

Lynn slept in the front seat, and Cheryl behind her in the rear seat. About 10 miles from home I was driving along a small B road into a village on the outskirts of the market town of Bishop Auckland, when without warning a car pulled across in front of me trying to get to a petrol station. I remember thinking 'fuck' and knowing at that point there was no way of avoiding the eventual impact.

The noise of the impact was something I could never have imagined, having never been in a crash before. The heat from the airbag hitting me in the face was unexpected, as was the quiet immediately after the crash. We came to a stop in a hedge that bordered a small bungalow neighbouring the petrol station. My immediate thought was to get everyone out of the car. For some bizarre reason, and probably some subliminal fear I was concerned about the car catching fire. I looked across at Lynn whose face was bloodied, she was clearly in pain from what we later found out was a broken shoulder. Her side of the car was totally embedded in the hedge, I helped her across the driver seat and out of the car, I was shouting to Cheryl to get out of the car but there was little movement from the rear of the car. I went in to get Cheryl but she was clearly unconscious.

In the time-lapse from freeing Lynn, a man and woman had appeared, the gentleman went into the back of the car to see to Cheryl while I went back to Lynn who was sitting at the roadside being comforted by the lady. The lady informed me that her travelling companion who was tending to Cheryl was in fact a dentist, this gave me some comfort. The emergency services soon arrived and went to see the gentleman tending to Cheryl. Before the ambulance got to her, he informed me that her pulse was not good and her blood pressure appeared to be dropping. In hindsight, I have often wondered if that was his way of saying 'you are losing your daughter'.

In all the activity, another couple was at the scene helping where possible as well as the emergency services. Throughout this whole chaotic episode, Lynn was clearly in distress and pain, and I tried my best to comfort her. Within minutes the news was broken to me that Cheryl had passed away at the scene, still in the back of the car. I went straight to Lynn to break the news. She let out a noise that I'm guessing only a mother can in learning that she has lost a child, as I looked up at the kind people who had come to offer help they were clearly very upset.

We were escorted to the ambulance, and we both felt we could not leave Cheryl at the scene. I had a strange sense of abandonment that felt terrible. On the way to the ambulance we had to walk past the guy who had caused the accident, I simply said: "My daughter is dead". I have analysed this statement a lot over the years, and I'm convinced I said that because I felt that was what I had to say in that situation, I have also regretted the statement. Prior to that moment, had somebody asked what would I do if someone had killed my child, like many, my response would likely have been that I would kill them. At that moment, I think that was the only response I could have mustered.

The journey to the hospital was both emotional and empty. When we arrived at the hospital there was a full team waiting to make sure we were OK. I had no injuries other than what was going on inside of my head.

While Lynn was being treated I was left with the daunting task of phoning family to give the news. I phoned Lynn's mother's home. Betty my mother-in-law answered. "Betty, we've been involved in a bad accident." "How is everyone?", Betty asked. "Lynn has hurt her shoulder and back but will be fine, but Cheryl…" I hesitated and struggled for what to say, as most grieving people will tell you the word dead is way too cold and final. "It's the worst possible Betty. She's gone" The line fell silent before Betty asked where we were, she told me she would get Lynn's father, Albert, and make the 15-mile trip to the hospital immediately. Next, I phoned my parents house, thankfully the phone was answered by my younger sister, Anita. My relationship with Anita has always been strange. I don't think either of us would describe each other as being particularly close, however, we are a very pragmatic type of family, and on this occasion, that disposition worked well. "We've had a crash and Lynn's hurt but OK, but… Cheryl's gone."

"What do you mean 'gone?" she replied. I couldn't put into words what 'gone' meant, but she eventually understood what I was trying to say. I asked if she could bring Lee through to the hospital and I would break the news to him there.

My inability to say 'dead' was my first stage of grief, ***denial****. That coupled with the numbness and avoidance I experienced during the early hours following the accident. It took me years to say dead, and even today it feels very uncomfortable. This proves that the stages of grief can stay with you for many years with varying degrees of emotional discomfort. Such a small word that can be incredibly emotionally impactful.*

The aftermath of the accident in the hospital was a mixture of chaos and confusion with medical staff wanting to look at both myself and my wife Lynn. I hadn't realised that when the hospital received the call that there had been a road traffic accident, they had a team waiting to deal with whatever injuries may present. I recall at the point of admission things seemed to be happening very quickly, and my brain was racing. I was numb to feelings, but hyper alert to everything that was happening around me, I had a strong sense of needing to engage where possible, almost denying the knowledge and images that my brain had been asked to process regarding the loss of my daughter. I wouldn't accept medical intervention for myself, I felt physically numb as well as emotionally numb. My daughter was dead and my wife was clearly in pain, I simply didn't feel worthy of attention. I did however have an overwhelming sense of duty to tell the extended family despite it being the last thing I wanted to do. I was clearly in a state of denial despite the overwhelming evidence to the contrary, my brain was taking measures to protect me from the catastrophic information it was being fed and having to process into a manageable order. The brain is an amazing tool.

On the evening of the accident, I was sat in the hospital ward completely bewildered and desperately trying to make sense of my situation. A nurse came up to me and handed me an A4 piece of paper with the title 'dealing with grief', what is grief was my immediate thought. I'd obviously heard of grief but had no real idea what its true meaning was, or how impactful it could be. I looked through the stages of grief that were clearly bullet pointed to see where I was on this new found route to emotional freedom. I viewed the stages as a tick list that I could use to measure when I would feel better, or when the immeasurable pain would lift. I looked at the five stages grief, Denial-Anger-Bargaining-Depression and finally Acceptance to see how many I could tick off in the 8 hours I had been a grieving parent! I couldn't really relate to any feelings of depression, does this mean I have found a way through the other stages without even realizing it? So may questions, so few answers, despite the best intentions of the kind nurse the information had only added to the confusion I was already feeling. With the knowledge I have today this would have been an excellent point for emotional intervention. How comforting it would have been for someone to sit me down and help me with my feelings, considering what I had just experienced. A little insight as to what may lie ahead or a telephone number of someone who may be able to help or support me over the coming days weeks and months.

Lynn was transferred from the A&E area to a ward where I joined her. Lynn's parents were first to arrive, I remember seeing Albert in a small waiting room, head bowed and understandably upset. We chatted and I explained that everything happened so fast and was so unexpected that there was nothing I could do. Anita arrived shortly afterward. She had broken the news to Lee on the way to the hospital. To this day, I owe Anita a huge debt of thanks for the way she handled the whole situation, including breaking the news to my parents and keeping them at home rather than them travelling through to the hospital.

The hospital was a whole world of mixed emotions, Lynn was put into a side room and I was allowed to stay with her for the four days she remained in hospital. I was terrified to leave, and I have huge pangs of guilt that I assumed Lee would be OK being looked after by his grandparents and my sister, while I 'took care of things' at the hospital.

The Chapel of Rest became something of a sanctuary where we could visit Cheryl and fuel our denial. Lee's first visit to the Chapel of Rest was particularly harrowing. He was cut to the core and cried uncontrollably as he looked for answers. Lee made many visits to the chapel. This was something that we didn't discourage in the hope it would help him find closure. For what did I know at this point? I have a wife in hospital, I'm in hospital at her side, my son is with my parents and sister. Two families are torn apart, and I have a child in a mortuary, what do I do next?

The Deal

*Yet again the daily visits to the chapel of rest were a source of great comfort and yet more evidence of **denial**, it felt as though I still had a connection and as long as that connection remained, then so did Cheryl!*

I was suddenly faced with a whole raft of problems that I had never begun to consider. What happens with Cheryl now? There would be a funeral, but who arranged that? Again, my sister came through by giving me the number of a school friend who had gone on to become an undertaker. On meeting Stuart, I was immediately put at ease. He took what appeared to me to be a mountain of a problem out of my hands and allowed me to focus on mine and my families grief.

Through Stuart, I met Rev John Bell. John was the vicar of my local parish Church, St Cuthbert's in the City of Durham. On first impressions, I recall him having a welcoming face and a warm approach to death. He shared his experience of losing a nephew and the impact that had on his whole family, as the conversation progressed I could feel a connection with my faith. It was arguably a stage of denial as I reached out for any form of connection with Cheryl, but whatever it was I wasn't going to pass it up as I was in desperate need of something. Before leaving we said a prayer that added warmth.

This isn't a religious journey as my views have swayed many times over the years, but it is part of my journey and should be included. *Do I have faith?* Yes, *what is your faith in?* I haven't got a clue. What I do know is that at my lowest point I did a deal with a Higher Power,: "Show me the way, show me what you want me to do, and I'll do it". In return, I just wanted to know that Cheryl was OK. I needed some direction as I didn't have a clue. Little did I know at the time, but the deal I made was the start of a more than 20-year journey involving so many characters and emotions that I could never have known even existed.

*This was probably the first time I entered the **bargaining** stage of my grief. The willingness to do whatever it would take to ensure Cheryl was OK and that connection could continue with me in my fatherly role.*

A strange thing happened during those early days in the hospital, as I walked around communal areas for a change of scenery I would occasionally think I had caught glimpses of Cheryl. If I saw a fair-haired girl of similar age from behind, my mind would immediately play a trick on me, although I knew this wasn't possible I can't deny enjoying that split-second of comfort. Another thing I had not accounted for was how I would react to sudden unexpected movements after being in a high-impact collision. My first experience was a pair of automatic double rubber doors that opened as I approached. I was wandering along in a daze and the mechanical action of the doors opening made me sink to my knees in shock, I had never experienced anything like that uncontrolled reaction before, or the embarrassment that followed!

*As I read this I can remember thinking I could see Cheryl on so many occasions, that craving for her presence fueled my **denial**. On a long haul flight I felt immense comfort from a fair hared female three rows in front that reminded me of Cheryl from behind. As I write this I question my sanity at that time, but I come back to the stages of grief and the need to acknowledge them rather than dismiss them.*

As I approached home for the first time following the accident my long-time friend Steven Patterson was there, he was a welcome face, and being a firefighter I felt as though I could talk about the accident a little more. Most parents would feel distraught at the prospect of witnessing their child's death and quite rightly so. I on the other hand feel comfort in witnessing the whole experience. That sounds odd so, let me explain. On the day of the accident, Steven was meant to be on shift. If I hadn't been there and Steven had told me Cheryl had passed away peacefully, would I have believed him? Probably not. Not because Steven's a liar, simply because it's human nature to protect those that you care about, and I would always have wondered if he was holding something back to protect me.

The house felt empty and cold, despite it being a bright September day. We immediately went to Cheryl's room and the feelings were overwhelming. We could touch and smell clothes that still held her scent. The pictures on the walls reminded me of countless conversations and jokes we had shared. Her mother sat broken "She was perfect..." she kept on repeating, "...she was".

Another issue for me was the attention my new role as a grieving parent would receive. Nobody knows how to respond in these situations, do I smile at the grieving parent, offer condolences, or simply ignore or avoid. As anti-social or ungrateful as this may sound, I would have preferred that latter. I was struggling to deal with my own emotions and thoughts without being burdened with someone else's. I wanted to be me, I didn't want to be defined as a grieving parent. I hadn't achieved a lot in my life, but I didn't want to be simply known as "Steve Vasey, he lost his daughter you know..." I decided to face it head-on by walking everywhere or cycling. I was still unsure about driving following the accident. Some people half-smiled, others offered sympathy, interestingly one lady who herself had lost a child to cancer admitted thinking about ignoring me, but decided to offer condolences. It was a strange time. I was also confused about what people felt I should do? Would they expect me to be locked away grieving, is that the right thing to do? Would they think I didn't care by choosing to face it head-on, as if I'd miraculously recovered: "She couldn't have meant that much to him...". It was all madness, and very draining. It was a theatre within my head with a director who wasn't fit for the job – chaos!

The time between death and burial was terrible. You are in limbo. You are dealing with practicalities that can be a refreshing escape, while not feeling fully able to grieve because the person you have lost is still physically present and not yet officially put to rest. I was getting comfort from my newfound faith. I would pray constantly asking for Cheryl to be cared for, and feeling a real sense of connection that allowed me some control over the separation process. The funeral was horrible, standing room only and attended by so many of Cheryl's young friends. Children shouldn't have to be exposed to death and loss in this way. A lasting memory was seeing one of her friends crying uncontrollably as we walked out after the service. I also remember another close friend of Cheryl, Rebecca, walking to her open grave and throwing in a teddy bear, and her Mam Ellen pulling her back as she'd caught sight of the coffin in the grave. I remember little else from that day, other than an overwhelming smell of lilacs around the home and church. I still get a nasty trigger from the smell of lilacs to this day.

Transference *is an interesting theory that can thread its way through a grieving process. You may hear a song that immediately transfers you to a place or time with good or bad memories. You may meet someone who reminds you of someone else, you may transfer the feelings of the old person to the new person, which can have both good or bad results. I learned many years later that this process was called transference. In this instance for me it was Lilacs, if they are in a building I may not instantly recognize the smell but I will* *have a dip in mood. It is only when I narrow the culprit down to lilacs that I understand the transference of feelings to the day of Cheryl's funeral.*

As with everything since the accident, there were so many questions and very few answers. The days rolled by and my only sanctuary was praying to help with my connection to Cheryl, which led to me attending church. The church was a welcoming place where I could be me, I felt almost normal, although for me to end up in a church was the most un normal thing imaginable pre-accident. The church allowed me to explore the connection between the old me, and the new me. I was still constantly asking for direction, although I got peace from being sat in a congregation and being surrounded by caring people. It never felt this was my path.

*Praying became such an integral part of my emotional wellbeing. On one level it was **denial**, attempting to reconnected with Cheryl by whatever means possible. On another level it was an opportunity to have some internal dialogue, and opportunity to explore my feelings and explore routes from the weight of feelings I was carrying around with me, I would liken it to self-counselling.*

Of course, there will never be a return to what I thought of as normal, how could there be? One of the main pieces of my life was now missing. I needed to resume some sort of normality quickly, and the first thing I did was return to work. Work at the time was a large building site just outside of York where we were installing the heating. The building was for the Rowntree family who were building it as a respite centre for people with various disabilities. The site was very much in its early stages with no roads and various site cabins located around the new construction where companies like ours would store their equipment. It was quite a friendly site of approximately 100 construction workers. On my first day back, I parked my car in the designated compound, collected my bag from the backseat, and made my way to our cabin. This was a walk I had run through my head so many times and was dreading. My stomach was churning. Thankfully, arriving early had ensured there would only be a handful of workers milling around which was fine.

I felt as though everyone knew what had happened. I worried what their reactions would be in this macho environment where we didn't do feelings. When I got with the squad I worked with, nobody knew what to say other than, "hi". It was really awkward. The hours turned into days, and then weeks, without the accident ever being spoken about. It felt as though working life was slowly feeling a little more normal.

*It is interesting that I have never felt **anger** towards the guy who caused the accident. I have explored this so often and wondered whether that stage had manifested itself in some other way. The most natural feeling pre accident would have been to hate the guy, or even want to cause him harm. Yet here I was feeling nothing, simply empty. I did wonder if I could relate to his part in the accident because like many drivers I had almost caused an accident myself through complacency, thankfully without incident. I simply don't know, I was so drained of energy at that point in time perhaps my sub conscious had taken over not allowing me to use valuable energy on such a futile emotion as anger.*

A few weeks had past and I was having a particularly difficult day with flashbacks and thoughts of Cheryl. About mid-afternoon, I decided to go into the large loft area where I knew nobody would be working just to have some time alone and gather my thoughts. I climbed the temporary steps and eased back the hatch and stepped into the loft and replaced the hatch behind me. Out of the darkness came a voice, "hello". I put on my light and saw the ventilation guy sitting on some timber. I asked if he was OK? to which he replied: "yea mate, I'm just skiving till home time and my lift arrives." He smiled got up then climbed from the loft. On the following Monday, the guy he worked with came on-site in some distress. He explained how he'd gone to pick up his colleague but the street where he lived was cordoned off with police tape, and there were police officers and people in white overalls wandering all over the street. He asked a neighbor what was going on and she told him his colleague, the one I disturbed in the loft had murdered his wife the evening before. This only goes to show that you never know, and with men perhaps more so as we never talk as openly as we ought to about our feelings. The resulting gossip after this event took the spotlight off me, two days later an ambulance pulled onto the site and the assistant site manager was taken from his office/cabin and led to the waiting ambulance, he'd had a breakdown at work. You really don't know what is going on in people's minds, unless they share.

I had no idea where my path was, I had no idea how I was going to survive the feelings and emotions that consumed my every waking hour. Cheryl would crash into my thoughts unannounced overwhelming me and causing such terrible pain. When it wasn't that, it was reliving the impact of the crash over and over and trying to close it out of my mind. It was around this time during the first month of returning to 'normal' life that I encountered an elderly lady at Church. I'm ashamed to admit that her name escapes me now, but I can remember feeling a sense of warmth when she spoke to me. She was in her late seventies with a caring attractive face, and well-spoken. This kind lady went on to tell me she had lost a child when she lived in Africa, had he still been alive he would have been 50 that year. This completely blew my mind. Fifty! That just seemed crazy, so long ago and yet still fresh in her conscious mind. She said that, since then, she had lost her husband but the pain of losing him was nothing like what she had experienced when losing her child. She went on to tell me that there would never be a day going by that she did not think of her son. At that point, I craved the thought of thinking of Cheryl daily, instead of every second of every day. She would crash into my thoughts unannounced inflicting overwhelming pain and sadness, I just didn't have a coping strategy to prevent this from happening. Worse still was reliving the accident over and over again which would make me wince with emotional discomfort. I was even developing coping strategies to cover the flashbacks, I might cough or move an arm at the point of impact or perhaps brush imaginary fluff from my trousers, all designed to mask involuntary movement brought about by severe emotional pain.

Years later I was diagnosed with PTSD (Post traumatic stress disorder). I'm very much against labels, but this label gave me a reason to start understanding my feelings and gave me something to address. I was becoming more and more exhausted and beginning to feel quite unwell. My anxiety was out of control, and I started worrying about everything. I just wanted simplicity, I had a business that caused no end of anxiety and a business partner who was unable to take up the slack from me wanting to ease off a little. At home, simple things around the home became a concern, the greatest of which were things that I felt were outside of my control. Things like bills, or anything financial I wanted to be rid of everything so that I could live a Spartan life where nothing could hurt me anymore. Thankfully, through this ordeal and future ones, harming myself was never an option. My sense of responsibility thankfully kept those thoughts at bay. At this stage, after such a loss, you crave other people's stories and their journeys to get a feel for where you are: how they suffered; how they came to terms; is there an easy route through this myriad of grief and pain? etc. I also became interested in near-death experiences to seek comfort in the belief that there was life beyond the grave, meaning Cheryl still existed and I was still connected.

*It was around this the time that another stage of grief was starting to play a major role in not just my recovery, but my emotional wellbeing, **Depression**. I had overwhelming feelings of sadness, irritability, and frustration over simple everyday matters. I was finding it increasingly difficult to concentrate on anything, and lack of sleep was becoming a major issue. I can remember feeling tortured by lack of sleep, which in turn tore into my resilience making me tearful and vulnerable. I would often feel exhausted and quite tearful when I was alone yet able to hide these feelings outwardly. Things that I had once enjoyed were now nothing more than a passing interest. Reading was virtually impossible, I simply couldn't concentrate for long enough to get any enjoyment, my mind would constantly drift. Everything became a struggle; I had no motivation to carry out anything. Interestingly part of my brain became incredibility creative, I could think of amazing business opportunities. However, this creative urge further compounded my feelings of worthlessness adding to my depression when I was unable to see them through. I simply lacked the motivation to do anything, however exciting it may seem in my thoughts. In a nutshell I was becoming increasingly unwell.*

Over the previous months and early years, I had been the strong one. I'd smiled supported, carried on, and been a textbook recovering grieving parent. However, now I looked around and everyone seemed to be moving on, I, on the other hand, felt as though mentally I was taking backward steps at an alarming rate, but didn't know what to do or who to tell, men are supposed to be strong. I was raised up to the age of 14 in an ex colliery house in a working-class area, before moving onto a council housing estate. Neither of these settings lends themselves to a young boy growing to express anything other than 'manly feelings' and certainly not feelings that show weakness. I don't wish to appear like the 'kid from the hood' but it was quite a tough environment and one where I felt comfortable. I think I felt comfortable because I'd created a tough enough exterior to survive and gain some respect. Fast forward to post-crash feelings and this thin macho veneer was being seriously tested, tested to the point where I just wanted to cast it aside and take my chances with what I had left to survive.

One day in particular I lay on the bed at home paralysed with fear and anxiety, I genuinely felt as though I had been glued to the bed, I was totally incapable of moving a single finger let alone a limb. I stared at the ceiling looking for an answer, not knowing where it would come from. I repeated over and over again: "just show me she's OK, that's all I need and I'll do whatever you want". I have no idea of how long I kept on repeating this sentence, all I knew was that the answer to that one question would help me more than anything else. Without warning, I was suddenly overwhelmed with an amazing sense of calm, almost warmth. It feels difficult to put into words how this feeling felt, other than peaceful. I felt at peace with myself and my immediate surroundings. I felt myself sink into the bed rather than being glued rigidly to the surface. At that point, I felt as though Cheryl was OK. As I write this I have a sense of how mad all this sounds but I can only say it as it happened. I have no idea who I thought I was speaking to, all I know is that my question was somehow answered, I also know I'd done a deal with something I didn't understand.

Was 'the deal' **bargaining***? Despite the overwhelming sense of intervention from a therapeutic perspective I certainly can't discount it.*

Having had this special moment, I felt I couldn't sit on my laurels. Part of the sentence was me saying 'I will do whatever you want'. I was so grateful for the respite I had gained and decided to go back to the figurative well for answers. I looked for direction, just something to point me in the direction I need to go to fulfil my end of the deal. I suppose I'd hoped for a flash of light and deep bellowing voice offering me some guidance, needless to say, that didn't happen.

What did happen was I saw a small advert in the church's monthly publication for Samaritans. The prospect of volunteering for an organisation like Samaritans was daunting. Despite feeling incredibly anxious, I decided to go along to a Samaritan open day. Out of respect for Samaritans who are a marvelous organisation based on anonymity, I will leave my experience there. What I will say is that I spent four wonderful years as a Samaritan volunteer, which demonstrated to me the power of listening. It challenged my insecurities, and I left a much stronger broader thinking person for the experience that pushed me well out of my comfort zone.

Eighteen months had passed since the accident and I was still being troubled with flashbacks, although they weren't as frequent, they were still causing me problems. I was able to mask them, but social situations could be difficult if one decided to make an appearance unannounced. The Samaritans had shown the power of listening, so I thought

I'd take my own advice and seek counselling. I made my appointment at the Road Centre in Durham. The name of the practice was merely coincidental to my accident, they focused on all aspects of emotional care. I'm not good at opening up and was very aware that this would become something of an emotional wrestling match unless I eased up a little and took a chance. At the time, I felt as though I had the whole world on my shoulders, the business, dealing with the grief, bills, and everyday household issues, at times it felt overwhelming. I can look back today and see that my concerns were nothing, but when your anxiety is going through the roof even the smallest everyday blip appears to be a potential disaster.

The first thing I wanted to address was the flashbacks. I was advised to treat them like a DVD and simply turn them off, for me that was never an option. What I did decide to do was relive them, concentrate on the event and see it through. Obviously, the pain involved in this approach is horrendous, however, the trade-off for me was seeing a reduction in the intensity of the flashbacks. What I did get from counselling was permission to slow down. On the face of things that may seem an easy fix, but in reality, it isn't. I had spent a lifetime 'being busy', in the grip of grief and anxiety the need to be busy increased to counteract all the perceived pitfalls I could see in front of me. This would see my working days grow longer and the diversity of tasks I would undertake increase. We also looked at some imagery where I could see myself as a young child tending a very small but immaculately kept garden, I was very defensive of the garden, but also very afraid and vulnerable. Whilst looking after my garden I was in the shadow of a large grey overbearing guard type figure, dressed like a soldier from a WW1 movie. Even today I think back to that image of a three or four-year-old me on my honkers looking at my garden then up to the threatening figure looming over me and wonder what, or who he was. Was he there to protect me, or prevent me from escaping?

Just as I saw 'the deal' as an intervention, the process of seeking counselling and sticking with it was certainly a positive intervention. My life was like a runaway train that I had little control over. Counselling allowed me time and space to gather my thoughts and assess my situation. I was also able to identify mechanisms that would trigger my anxiety, and areas of improvements I could make to help ease my situation, this mainly involved allowing myself to slow down. This intervention was key to me being able to navigate my way through the grieving process, without it I'm not sure I could have mustered the strength needed to build up my resilience allowing me to move forward. Someone was finally able to translate the bullet point stages of grief from the A4 paper handed to me by the nurse, into a reality that I was able to relate to and see myself within.

If I have to describe my relationship with Cheryl I tell of a time when I had no control of when she crashed into my thoughts, and her visits were not a particularly welcome experience due to the emotional pain it caused. Today things are very different. I imagine myself in a wonderful mature garden, and I invite Cheryl in. When she's there I think of the good times, happy times. Me keeping my end of the deal I made all those years ago when I asked if she was alright. It's a pleasant experience.

Dreams are another crazy thing. I have had so many dreams where I have had an awareness of a girl being present, a nice girl who is just there on the periphery of what's going on. It's only as I enter consciousness that I realise it's Cheryl, always in light clothes with her lovely fair hair. I have mixed feelings when I awake, part of me is so happy for feeling close to her, the other a little disappointed that we didn't talk. In rare dreams, she's spoken, nothing earth-shattering, just in line with general conversation. The only difficult dreams I have had are the ones when I dream it has all been a mistake and she's still with me. I can count on one hand the amount I have had like this, but again despite the obvious difficulty in the dream and the empty feeling when I realise nothing has changed, I'm still grateful for some sort of connection.

Part of my volunteering with Samaritans saw me involved in the Crisis open Christmas event in London. This event is held each Christmas when a large disused venue is taken over, staffed by various charitable organisations, then the doors are open to those who may find themselves homeless at Christmas time. There are hundreds of people using the venue, while they're there they can have warm meals, the chance to talk to someone, clothes, a haircut or see a Doctor, and ultimately have a safe bed for the night in the large hall. It's a truly wonderful event that deserves all the support it can get. It's also a valuable and humbling experience to be fortunate enough to volunteer.

I learned so much during my two visits, but the key learning was how much unsupported mental health can play in a person's descent to homelessness. I had conversations with some incredible guests who were bright, intelligent and articulate, then see them minutes or hours later when they were gripped with anxiety or psychosis, and they are virtually incoherent and could be seen as troublesome by people who had not had the pleasure of meeting their other-self.

I spoke to a former miner who had worked at Easington Colliery in County Durham. He had worked there while I worked in the area as a heating engineer for the local authority. He told me how the miners' strike in the 1980s had virtually ruined him, not only financially but emotionally. I had witnessed first-hand the devastation caused by the miner's strike, and how the soul was torn out of men, women, children, and communities. Today all these years after the strike those same communities are ravaged with substance misuse and crime, young people entering the job market are second or third-generation unemployed with very poor prospects or motivation. The chap I spoke to had gone through a difficult marriage breakup as his mental health failed to recover after the strike. He was a bitter man and clearly in conflict with not only himself but the world at large.

I spoke with a lady in her late 30s who was very articulate and well-spoken. She told me of choosing to come to the open Christmas rather than stay in her top-floor flat surrounded by drug dealers and violence. It was interesting to watch her emotional state deteriorate as the hours passed and she conversed with people who were obviously familiar to her. By the following morning, she was little more than a mumbling shell of the person I had spoken to the previous day. I could go on recounting stories of sadness and unattended suffering that I experienced. I left feeling hurt by the suffering I had witnessed, however, what I had gained was a sense of direction. I wasn't sure what form this direction would take but I knew there was an issue I could possibly help address.

In a strange and slightly worrying way I could identify with most of the guests I had spoken to. They were almost like lost soles trying to navigate their way through a similar process that I found myself in. It was concerning watching them desperately looking for something they had lost, and seeking solace with people in a similar predicament to themselves. I too found both reading and conversations with those who had experienced a similar situation to my own engrossing. Samaritans had a whole host of wonderful volunteers from all manner of backgrounds with a wide range of life experiences. I found the company of these people wonderful and insightful, especially those who had found the path from adversity. I was desperately searching for Acceptance, the final stage of my process.

While running my business, I was terrible for avoiding personal issues that involved paperwork. One of these issues was pensions. I tried to be interested but found the language and people selling it confusing and drab and chose not to engage. What I did do was look at my skill set and look for ways of utilising them to combat my pension problems. I decided to get a mortgage on a second property and rent it out in the hope that many years later it would be paid for and I would get a small income from the rent it generated. The added bonus was that I could buy a property requiring work and do the work myself as well as the maintenance once tenanted out. The plan worked well, so I decided to buy a house that I would convert into two flats. All of this happened some years prior to my accident, but the property did cause some anxiety when I worried about irrational potential problems that could arise.

Over the years I rented the property out it had become a revolving door process where tenants would move in, be unable to sustain a tenancy, then leave. Each time I felt this one may be different, but without support, the outcome was inevitable as they experience the utopia-to-despair cycle of having a roof over their head to not being able to cope. In the late nineties, I had a meeting to show a particular tenant around called Lara. Lara arrived with an older lady, she told me she was 16 and clearly heavily pregnant. Her pregnancy was exaggerated by her slight frame, and what looked like deflated posture. She told me she had been living in a neighboring town, although she was originally from the village where the house was located, and her mum also lived in the village. She was really chatty and engaging, she went on to explain that the lady with her was from the local teenage pregnancy unit. This is where things became challenging, a challenge that would repeat itself many times over the coming years. I found myself in a head and heart situation! My head was screaming, walk away, this will be nothing but trouble. She's young, with a baby, how will she cope and what about when young men realise she lives here and start coming to the house? What if she starts having parties and the house gets trashed? It wouldn't be the first time that had happened. Meanwhile, my heart was saying, take her on, she's really pleasant.

After some serious internal dialogue, what finally swung it was that she'd sought the support of the teenage pregnancy unit, which she didn't have to. Her mother lives close by for support, what more could she do? That sealed it, and Lara became a tenant.

As was always the case I was left feeling good and warm inside about the decision I had made, this inevitably happened when my heart won. This became the beginning of the homelessness charity I founded called Cornerstone Supported Housing and Counselling. Little did I know the next 20 years would see me working with a complex group of lost souls on my own, with no support or training. I made so many mistakes and worked with people I really had no right to become involved with like the schizophrenic, who nobody would acknowledge let alone work with. I had no idea I was forming what would go on to become a charity, but I did have a strong sense of direction. I trusted the deal implicitly. All these wonderfully colorful characters are what formed what Cornerstone is today.

*It is clear that I was slowly entering the **acceptance** phase of my process following Cheryl's death, I have purposely used the word death to challenge myself and yes 24 years later it is still uncomfortable. Acceptance is accepting the world where the person or thing you have lost no longer exists, and I felt more comfortable with this situation than at any time since the accident. I still had my moments of disbelief and anxiety, but with all the other elements of the grieving process gradually being addressed I felt a lot more comfortable in this new world. Recalling that time I view the stages of grief as a staircase that you need to climb, and at some point you will get a glimpse over the top of the staircase onto a new level. Hopefully that new level will be full of opportunities and hope, but in my case it is fair to say that I didn't have a lot of optimism, just a little hope in the direction my life was starting to take.*

At about this time I had enrolled on a college course studying counselling and psychotherapy. What I had learned through my experience was the power of listening. I was keen to explore myself further. It was also at this point I met one of the most influential people to impact my life. Sandra Dobson was the lecturer at college and instilled in me the benefits of positive feedback and treating each person as an individual. So much of Sandra's approach made me try harder, I felt valued, I felt part of something. It drove me to keep on going till I qualified four years later. For the first time in my life, I felt part of a system designed to educate and modified by a truly inspirational lady.

So much was changing in my life. My relationship with Cheryl was more balanced, where I could go to a place in my mind to visit her which was lovely, instead of the previous gut-wrenching intrusions. College was going well. I'd also made the decision to get out of my business and pursue a career that was more emotionally rewarding. The first step I made was running a telephone helpline for parents who were in distress. The work involved the mechanics of running a helpline while also offering emotional support and training to the amazing volunteers we had. I had to put faith in the deal I had made that day when I had lain paralysed with fear on the bed that everything would work out, and it did. I handed my business over to my business partner and became a part-time worker. The strange thing was that I had little doubt that things would work out, despite taking a significant drop in income and stepping into a new world so far removed from the building industry. My faith was rewarded with four great years working in a great team at Parentline.

A change that wasn't so welcome was the distance I was feeling from my wife Lynn. We had been growing apart as we healed differently from the trauma of losing Cheryl. In the early day's I felt I had to be strong for everyone, but as time moved on it felt as though everyone was moving on and I was stuck with these horrible flashbacks. I could never verbalise how it felt, and certainly never felt that my pain was worse than anyone else's. I don't know whether it was because I witnessed the accident unfold while Lynn and Cheryl slept, or the subsequent interviews by police and coroner's meetings. I just knew that my pain felt a little different. Lynn had suffered terribly emotionally as any grieving mother would, she described Cheryl as perfect, and to us she was. To this day, I share Lynn's pain and wish her every possible happiness in her future, she deserves it. As our marriage drew to a close we kept things as civil as possible and became another statistic of the relationships that end following the death of a child.

Lara was still living in my rented property and doing brilliantly. She had been with me for two years at this point and was by far the best tenant I had ever had. She was bright beyond her years, and through the brief conversations we had, I felt she had huge potential, she had a particular entrepreneurial quality about her.

I was slowly finding myself drawn to working or trying to support people who were marginalised. The Open Christmas event in London had made me view homelessness differently. I looked at issues leading to their situation. I looked at the people I had dealt with at Samaritans and Parentline, and the range of complex issues they presented with. I also reflected on the tenants I had dealt with who I had given the chance of a home. The initial euphoria of having their own home soon overwhelmed with the inability to sustain a tenancy. I decided to try and do something about it.

At this time, my business was no longer, having successfully handed it over to my partner, I had left Parentline, and had been working for a young carers charity in a neighboring town part-time. I loved the work at Eastern Ravens Trust, and the people I was fortunate to work with and support. My role was to work with families of young carers and try to make interventions where possible and offer support. I had consciously taken a part-time role knowing that I didn't need a huge amount of money to survive. I had stripped things back in my life, looked at what I felt was important, and what I could do without. Having stripped everything back I was now in a much less stressful situation, but also well-positioned to look at the housing part of my work to see what the best way may be to progress my thinking around homelessness. I am proud to say that I class my colleagues from Eastern Ravens as friends even to this day, the young people I helped care for are now grown up, some with families of their own who I am still in contact with.

*This was an important part of my recovery. I forced myself to take responsibility then take control. It was also a very dangerous time as I was clearly still suffering from **depression**, my mental health had improved significantly, but it was still impacting on my decision making. I had an overwhelming desire to become well at whatever cost, if that meant getting rid of everything to reduce stress then so be it. However, with the benefit of hindsight I can see that I would have traded anything for better mental health. To give myself credit I can see that some of the planning I was beginning to do would inevitably bring its own stresses which I didn't shy away from. Nevertheless, at this critical stage of the grieving process when you're almost at the top of the stairs the risks are still real. Some of the things I took out of my life could have benefitted me further down the road, I just felt that I couldn't carry their burden at that point in my recovery.*

A property came up for sale in the local high street of Willington in County Durham, and I decided to take a look and see if it was something I could work with. The building consisted of a tiny shop front with an adjoining door that took you through to the living quarters of the house. There were no rooms, there wasn't even a floor, just a drop of some 18" to a rubble and clay subfloor. When stood on the subfloor, if you looked up you could see all the way through the first floor to the underside of the roof tiles in the loft. No wall had plaster let alone doors, and the kitchen and bathroom were long gone. So here was a boarded-up shell that had been for sale for quite some time, on a busy street. Perfect!

The property was bought, and the work began. Working part-time allowed me the luxury of being able to spend more time at the property. Once again I never doubted the energy and motivation I would get from the deal I had done. What followed was nine months of challenging work, and countless questions from the local residents: "What's it going to be?" Who owns it? etc etc. I hedged around the questions about the building's eventual use to prevent unnecessary attention. I had already decided I would use the property to house three homeless people who would struggle to have their own tenancy, let alone keep it. The house was in a relatively small town where word would travel very fast, I decided the best way to move things forward with as little disruption as possible was to stay under the radar.

*This was another pivotal point in my recovery, and more evidence that I was beginning to feel more comfortable in the **acceptance** stage. Having tried to rid myself of anything that felt overly stressful, and this normally involved anything money related, the purchase of this property through a mortgage was a big emotional as well as financial step for me. I felt committed to the deal I had made and the journey I was on, this was evidenced by the hours I was putting into the work I was doing. Where I am today emotionally, I can see this was a natural progression and one that needed to be made, but in the emotional chaos I was experiencing at the time it felt huge. It felt like I was stepping back into the lion's den and facing the very things I had so painstakingly rid myself of. I was introducing risk back into my life, I was slowly growing stronger and so was my self-belief. Throughout the whole process I was constantly questioning myself and my resilience, yet here I was putting faith in myself and my ability to succeed. Underpinning the decisions I was making was the deal that I had done while paralised with anxiety on the bed, so was this me **bargaining**? I guess there has to be an element of that involved, but I know I had a will to succeed that bolstered my self belief. Perhaps my faith in the deal may have been a driver, but I believe this new found self belief through acceptance carried the whole project across the line.*

The original small shop was now, after the refurbishment, an office with vertical blinds that were constantly kept closed to prevent unwanted attention. I had made my proposed service known to Durham County Council, this would allow me to take referrals from people who had presented as homeless. As the paint was drying, we took our first referral, a young lad from Darlington. For a lot of years, the revenue wouldn't cover the outgoings, the shortfall was being paid by myself. This proved challenging on a personal level, but I had faith that if I kept on trying, things would fall into place. The months passed and I had taken several referrals, some stayed a few days then disappeared, others longer.

I knew the key to the venture's success was to not upset the local community, primarily through anti-social behavior. Word travelled fast through the community about our work, this inevitably resulted in some unwanted attention. The property was damaged, as was my car on numerous occasions. While I understood people's fear of the unknown, and that's what we were, I didn't feel the punishment matched the perceived crime.

As Cornerstone became known to other services, the referrals began to increase. This was not always a good thing, as some of the less reputable organisations tried to use me as a dumping ground and succeeded due to my misplaced trust and inexperience. The promise of ongoing support for the individual rarely materialised as they had reached their goal of moving the individual on, and claiming their fee from the government for a 'successful move on'. I vowed that this would never be how Cornerstone would run, and we wouldn't take on contracts that were aimed at easing government statistics whilst compromising the individual's current or future well-being. And we haven't!

*I became completely immersed in the work I was doing, this without doubt helped my mental health. It was a distraction with the benefit of positive outcomes. It eased my transition into **acceptance** and allowed acceptance to feel more doable. I wouldn't want the reader to feel this was the end of my grieving, it certainly wasn't. You constantly dip in and out the various stages, some days I would feel immense loss and start bargaining or feel depression clouding over me. Inevitably work and focus drew me back into normality and the acceptance stage would become prevalent.*

Being given the most chaotic clients on the books was incredibly challenging. Some had substance abuse issues, while others had significant entrenched emotional and mental health problems. They were clearly difficult to house on their own, but worse still together. This dynamic would occasionally result in parties or fallouts. I was still working part time, this meant getting to the Cornerstone house at 7am, leaving for work at 10am. Doing my paid work, then getting back to the Cornerstone house about 3pm and staying through to 7pm. This was obviously draining, but worse I was starting to feel like a policeman whose job it was to try and prevent anti-social behaviour, the 'cops and robbers' model I would later refer to it as. This model is difficult to manage, and I would constantly find this put huge stress on my relationship with the clients and my ability to support them effectively.

I soon realised that things worked better when you built a relationship and really got to know the clients so that you could acknowledge their achievements, however small. Two residents that joined the service after a year or two were Chris and Paul. Paul came first, a 25 year old broad Geordie with a very slight frame. He presented as quiet and quite shy, both personality traits proved to be obstacles over the coming years. Paul was referred through Tyneside probation service, he was difficult to house because he had a dog. Paul was prepared to stay homeless rather than give his dog up. I was told that he didn't have a significant criminal record, having recently been released from HMP Durham for non-payment of fines, the fines were for continually riding on the local Metro train service without paying. This was a theme with Paul in the years that followed, not wanting to take responsibility then becoming overwhelmed with regret and self-loathing from making the wrong choice. This was not exclusive to Paul and would re-appear with many clients over the years.

I would get up, visit the property, go to my daytime job then return to the property to check up. The consistent themes were, nobody would be awake during my morning visit and the place would be untidy, dishes left out, signs of drinking, alcohol spills and the smell of stale booze. I would go to work and on returning, the lads would be up and sitting around or perhaps attending appointments. By this time, they had already started to drink. They were totally unmotivated, and by offering accommodation I had only started to meet their basic needs. I didn't feel I was using any of the skills I had learned, and I was basically enabling them to live their lives this way. I would wonder what would happen if I didn't call in, would I be missed?

This routine made me feel angry. Angry at myself for not being more assertive, angry at the clients for not showing some respect, or acknowledging that we were all in this together. I couldn't do it alone, I needed their help. I wasn't their keeper, something clearly had to change. I would often feel sorry for myself which was neither healthy or justified. There were so many uncertainties, all I knew is that I had to keep my faith in the belief that I would be helped through the process.

Although I would occasionally use counselling skills, this clearly wasn't enough. It would help ease an immediate crisis but felt ineffective in creating a long-term client plan. They also found the intensity of a traditional counselling session too invasive, this threatened the supportive relationship I had with them.

Around this time, I had two long-term clients. Paul who I have previously mentioned and Chris. Both were alcohol dependent, but Paul's was more choice-based. Paul could go without alcohol for days, then drink for two days solid. I rarely saw Paul drunk, however, there was a clear difference between the sober and the drunk Paul. I also had Chris. Unlike Paul, Chris was drink-dependent and without alcohol in his system, he would often have a fit. Whilst I never witnessed a fit first hand, others had and it was disturbing and lasted up to a minute. Chris had a good awareness of his addiction and would budget accordingly, he was very intelligent and artistic and had previously ran his own successful business. On the very rare occasions, he would miscalculate his finances he would come to me shaking almost uncontrollably. Like Paul, his choice of drink would be super strength cheap cider in a plastic bottle. I have never known anyone buy one of these drinks for a 'normal' social activity, they always seemed to be used to self-medicate an addiction. The brand names alone are enough to put general shoppers off buying them such is the stigma attached, yet they are sold off shelves the length and breadth of the country. Even the addicts have a standing joke between themselves that the drink has never seen an apple.

After much thought, I decided a small workshop where we could build things together could to be the way forward. We had a small space in the rear yard that would be big enough to build an 8x6 shed to start us off. We were in the grip of winter and the first problem I came across was laying the concrete base. There was a severe frost and freezing conditions which wouldn't allow me to put the concrete down, however, I had a slight break in conditions that were long enough to get the base laid. Of the three clients, Paul was on a week-long course that he had to attend to prevent his benefits from being stopped. Chris was only effective in the one-hour window of opportunity when he first woke up before his alcohol consumption would start to take effect. Interestingly I only ever saw Chris drunk once in almost two years.

My third client was a young lad called Michael. Michael was only twenty and had been with me a few months. Michael's issues were anti-social behavior and getting on the wrong side of the law. As a child, he'd always been in scrapes with police, having to attend special schools that could deal with his behavior. Like many people we deal with, Michael had decided to self-medicate swapping the prescribed medication of Ritalin, for the street medication of cannabis. Both had a calming influence, but one was way cooler to use, made even cooler because it was illegal. I'm not a believer in legalising cannabis, mainly because I have witnessed first-hand the long-term effects of its use, and misuse. Michael was very much in the paranoid phase of its misuse even when not under the influence. This would predictably lead to depression and unnecessary confrontations born from his paranoia. Despite all of this Michael had worked and wanted to work. His father worked in the dales on a small piece of land and helped on local caravan sites, Michael would help his father and looked up to him. I tapped into Michael's willingness, and he helped me lay the concrete and later erect the shed that would form our first workshop.

*I was edging deeper into the **acceptance** phase. I was making longer term plans and more importantly implementing them and seeing them through. I was still prone to occasional bouts of **depression**, but thankfully they were fleeting and quite easy to rationalise my way through.*

I felt I now had direction. I could house people and offer a learning experience that would hopefully help empower them and raise their aspirations. Several years had passed since losing Cheryl when I was contacted by a local charitable Hub called 2D. They had heard of what I was doing and were interested to know if there was anything they could do to help. My meeting was with Phil Davies. Phil was interested to know how I was financing the work that we were doing and why I hadn't considered becoming a charity. The straight answer was "what defines or even is a charity" I knew of the big charities some of whom I'd volunteered for, but had no idea who the small charities were and why they would even exist as charities. After a lengthy and I'm sure painful conversation for Phil he explained how we had charitable objectives, and how if we became a charity we could then apply for grant funding to support our work. The idea of getting 'money for nothing' as I saw it was appealing, but totally against my working ethic of 'an honest day's work for an honest day's pay' I would later find out that it certainly wasn't money for nothing, and the outcomes needed from grant funders were incredibly hard earned! I was clearly a work in progress. However, the advantage I had was that I already had a working charitable model that I could evidence to the Charity Commission and potential funders to let them see what we could achieve together.

Cheryl with her cousin Jill.

Cornerstones head office

Giving my Stepdaughter Pip away on her wedding day.

Me and my twin grandaughters Beaux and Charlie

My step daughters Pip and Nicky

My son Lee with my twin grandaughters Beaux and Charlie

Some of our work in the community

Just when I thought it was safe to relax

Kate is someone I met through my work, I found her bright bubbly, and a little bit annoying. Her feelings were similar toward me, although I'm not as sure about being bright and bubbly. Kate worked in a rehab as a councilor where I was doing some volunteering to gain experience. I think we were both a bit awkward, especially when we realised our feelings towards each other might be changing. But change they did and over time we found ourselves in a relationship. Along with Kate came two beautiful girls, Nicky & Pip. I found my life taking a bit of a back seat and suddenly I felt valued and dare I say happy! Lee got on with Kate and the girls, which was very important to me given what he had been through. Things were going great, I had my own place and Kate had hers. Occasionally we would spend time at each other's home, and often the kids would tag along. Seven months into the relationship, Kate went to her GP to enquire about a small pea-sized lump on her neck. The Doctor referred her to the hospital to make sure everything was OK and I agreed to accompany her. After the tests, we went home, at 6pm that evening the consultant phoned home and asked us to call back the following day. "Mrs Morson, the lump on your neck is secondary cancer. It is in your respiratory system and travelling" It was one of those situations where time seemed to stand still. Kate immediately started to ask relevant questions, while I was dumbstruck. What followed was two years of serious invasive surgery, brutal radiotherapy, and a lot of recovery. Thankfully pulling together as a family saw us through.

Kates diagnosis plunged me back into the grieving process, I felt totally out of control. Even with my new found knowledge I felt myself dipping in and out of stages with frightening regularity. It also dragged Cheryl back onto the scene, as well as some of the feelings I was still struggling with in relation to her death. I managed to hide my feelings and emotions from everyone, roll my sleeves up and get stuck in! I was looking for signs that things would be OK, if I found a parking space at the hospital that was a good sign for example. I began bargaining all over again 'let her get through this and I will devote myself further to what you want me to do', 'please take everything I own, just allow this whole distressing situation to have a positive outcome'. I immediately went into work mode, I never missed a hospital appointment and listened to every single word the various consultants would say and hang on to many of those words. Every positive word I would grab with both hands and put into my subconscious bank and relay back to Kate when we were home. By contrast Kate could only hear the negatives which offered a fair balance when we would share our different perspectives. Kate is now 17 years clear of cancer and she dealt with the whole unpleasant experience with great courage. Her children have both said that they have little recollection of the pain and suffering Kate went through. I take this as a complement that I carried out my role in Kate's recovery quite well, I protected them from all the unpleasantness that comes with a cancer diagnosis as severe as Kate's. The whole situation was a stark reminder of just how fragile I am and stopped me getting too far ahead of myself with the charity.

Ashley

Ashley was a young woman who had been brought to our project by her emotionally drained mother. This was unusual as clients had, as a rule, burnt all their bridges with family and were more often referred into our service by the police or other statutory organisations. Ashley wasn't your stereotypical client. She was attractive, well presented, and had an engaging personality. Ashley had two daughters who were in the care of her mother and father. Ashley had a long relationship with substance misuse, like many clients she had been led into that life through a relationship that was incredibly toxic.

Ashley's mother once told me that attending parents evenings with Ashley when she was at school was a pleasure. Teachers were full of praise for her politeness and eagerness to engage in classes. At 14 she met an older boy who would go on to become her boyfriend. He was a drug user. Her mother once said to me that she had felt that she lost Ashley then. She became obsessed with this young man and slowly drifted into his world. This situation isn't uncommon and raises an ongoing issue I have whereby parents are being blamed for their child's downfall. Ashley had everything, a loving family, comfortable home. An extended family who loved her dearly.

Ashley's time with us was personally rewarding, she had an emotional vulnerability that was both endearing and worrying. She would hang onto other people within the service and mirror their behavior in the hope of gaining their acceptance. She was never rude to staff and very appreciative of the support she was given. Ashley had an underlying health condition, diabetes. Ashley would spend most weekends with her parents and daughters on a nearby holiday caravan site where the family had a permanently sited caravan. One Friday evening I got a call from Ashley's mother asking if I had seen Ashley, which I hadn't. Her mother's concern surrounded Ashley's diabetes medication which she feared she may not have.

On Sunday afternoon I received a blunt uncaring call from a police officer 'Is that Steve Vasey, Ashley is dead, and we will need access to her property' I was totally gob smacked, not just at the unfeeling delivery from the police officer, but also that Ashley had died. Once again, 32 years old, a life ahead of her, and now dead. I'm sure my shock registered with the police officer and his tone softened when he realised the impact his statement had had on me. I'm still in touch with Ashley's parents and her daughters are growing into fine young women. The loss of Ashley impacted upon me quite badly, I got terrible transference to my situation with Cheryl. Her Mother is such a kind soul, to witness her suffering was and is terrible. Any parent of a child in the grip of substance misuse gets my respect, and pity. I often liken it to having a toddler who never grows up, such is their vulnerability and unpredictability. Ashley's parents and family were an enormous support to her, whatever the temptation to cut her loose they maintained a connection while also providing a secure base and family environment for her children. They rightly in my opinion focused on the wellbeing of their grandchildren while acting as a buffer for Ashley, as did their extended family. Ashley loved her mother dearly. Such a sad ending, the punishment doesn't fit the crime.

Regarding Ashley, it may be worth mentioning a new strand to our work. Historically we had always worked with men. This was a demand issue as 98% of our referrals were for male clients, and secondly, we weren't equipped to cater to the challenges that we faced working with women. At the time, we had two members of staff, myself and a volunteer Phil Hardy who found us through 2D the charity support organisation I mentioned earlier. He later became a full staff member. Neither of us had a real problem dealing with the difficult conversations we sometimes had daily with the male clients, however when we had females the dynamic shifted. Their behavior was often equally as challenging as that of our male clients, and sometimes worse. Yet, I was unable to have the type of difficult conversation that I had with the male clients that might have appeared quite confrontational from the outside. Whether this was a generational issue where I felt uncomfortable having a heated conversation with a woman, or whether I simply didn't have the skills, it was clearly a flawed dynamic within our charity.

What I did know, was that of the six female referrals we had taken over the previous four years, only three were still alive. The fact that the deaths didn't occur during the women's time with us, except for Ashley was irrelevant. What was relevant was the vulnerability of this particular client group. In many ways I think of the female service as Ashley's legacy, she was a strong driver to implement the service that so many women have benefitted from. Thanks Ashley.

The Charity goes from strength to strength

As the charity grew and employed more staff I worked on the balance between male and female staff knowing that our goal would be to gradually introduce more female clients who would receive the level of support that would allow them to grow and reach their potential in a supported manner. I am proud to say that today we have achieved that and have a dedicated female arm to our work.

Our first female employee was Melissa. Melissa was perfect for the role, funny, engaging and most importantly aware of her own vulnerabilities and lived experience. The female clients picked up on this and allowed her to grow into her role. At that time we had a female client called Debra, Debra could be verbally volatile and could see through someone if she felt they weren't being honest with her. Melissa and Debra hit it off immediately which lay the foundations for the female service within the charity. I love watching our clients grow, it is one of the many pleasures I have in my life today. But there is something special about seeing a woman referred into Cornerstone from a difficult situation progress. Watching her self-esteem grow and her stature within Cornerstone, all with the help and dedication of our excellent support staff. I am also proud to say that Cornerstone has employed many of its ex clients and helped them gain access to education. For some this process works for others we have planted seeds for a later date.

Like most things I tend to self-analyse nearly every situation I find myself in, the female part of our work was no different. Do I enjoy this side of our work because of some desire to stay reconnected with Cheryl? Does working with females help me re-enact the parental guidance that was taken away from me when Cheryl died? To answer both truthfully, I don't really know. I would be naïve to believe that on occasion I haven't felt transference, or the need to go that little bit further because I want to feel valued in a paternal sense from the recipient. It's such a minefield of thoughts and emotions when I allow myself to delve too deep and start to over analyse my every action. It's easier to say Cheryl, and the deal I did drive me every day to hopefully make a positive difference to other people's lives. In doing so I hope and often feel it is having a positive impact on my own emotional wellbeing.

For most grieving people the anniversary of your loved ones passing is a day, or weeks worth of challenges. With the advent of social media everyone's grief seems much more visible as they can use the written word and images to express their pain while using the computer screen as their shield. Mine has been different. I have never put flowers at Cheryl's graveside nor put anything on social media, I have simply never felt that I needed to. That isn't aimed at taking anything away from those who may do the opposite, it's simply an example of how we all express ourselves differently. I feel I can close my eyes and say a few words to myself about my love for Cheryl, and that is it. I've never felt the need or desire to project these feelings onto others, I simply don't feel I have to, I know what my relationship with Cheryl is, and it's quite personal. Likewise, I have gone to Cheryl's graveside for the last twenty odd years on significant dates to say a few words, look at the flowers and cards, and leave. This is in stark contrast to the early days weeks and months when a week wouldn't pass without me being graveside. I always return a week or so later to clear away the dying flowers and clean Cheryl's headstone. I was on holiday one year and wasn't able to get back to tidy things away for three weeks. On my return, the grave was a terrible mess of dead and dying flowers. I wondered what would happen if I didn't tidy away every year, or is this simply the pragmatic me looking for a purpose and this process feeds that need.

Something I found challenging in the early days of social media was Cheryl's friends from school expressing their feelings of loss on her anniversary, they still do this to this day. Back then I felt their pain, and it concerned me that despite being young women making their own way in the world, they still harbored this pain for Cheryl. Throughout the whole process I always felt the pain others were experiencing exasperated my own. I inwardly complain about having to clear the grave each year. One thing I know for sure is that if one day I went to tidy things up and someone had beaten me to it, I'm pretty sure it would hurt. I have now come to terms with this being my way of showing grief in a silent practical way, perhaps similar to those who choose to do it in a more public way. We all find comfort in different ways, there is no right or wrong. We adopt whatever method necessary to get ourselves through incredibly stressful situations. If that method works for you and doesn't adversely affect anyone else, then it's right.

This February was a challenging time for me and my family with the death of my Father, it was also a milestone in my recovery as a grieving parent. On the 17th of February, I sat down to have my breakfast and opened my Facebook account. I was shocked to read Happy birthday Cheryl, still love you loads and miss you, a message from one of her friends. I had forgotten! To the world outside, this wouldn't have meant anything because nobody would have known. But I knew. As per usual I immediately went into self analysing mode to understand how it had made me feel, and what I should do. Nothing! I would do absolutely nothing. Had I moved on? I felt little guilt. The same as not publicly demonstrating my grief, I eventually took this as a sign of progression. I didn't have to prove anything to myself, let alone punish myself for allowing it to slip my mind. What would Cheryl say? Yet more internal dialogue. Probably to 'carry on and stop worrying about it' I got past it. In the week leading up to Cheryl's birthday I had thought about it several times, thinking of how old she would have been. Would she have married, what about children? So many questions, so few answers, but that moment when I had to be reminded that it was her birthday I took as another example of my acceptance of the physical world where Cheryl no longer existed. However, she is still very much in my emotional world, and her legacy still lives on in the work that I do.

The deal I did all those years ago–has never let me down. I feel that I've maintained my side of the deal, despite wavering from time to time. I'm still here to tell the story with what most people would regard as a successful charity, which would suggest the other side of the deal-making process has held up their end of the deal as well. But who was the deal with? You hear of people who have gone through the 12-step programme for addiction talk about 'God' or their 'higher power'. Both of which I'm reliably informed relate to your other self or a self that has for so long controlled the rest of your being and thought making process. Part of the deal the 12-stepper will make is that they are powerless to this Higher Being, this enables them to hand themselves over to the programme to begin their recovery. Is this what I did? That day when I lay in bed frozen with anxiety, was I subconsciously acknowledging that I was finished. Was this the process of me handing myself over to a Higher Power?

The next question must be, was the Higher Power internal or external? I have mulled over this question so many times over the years. The few people I have told think it is external, particularly those who have faith. Those who are spiritual also tend to think it was an external intervention. My view is that I believe it was a combination of the two. That day I was literally finished, I had no inner resilience to pull me out of the pit of despair I found myself in. I needed an intervention to bolster what little strength I had, and it happened. Was it God? I suppose the bigger question is, what is God? And that's a route I feel unqualified to go down to find my answer. All I can share is that I felt something, something bigger than me. Something that was able to take control of the downward spiral I found myself in and somehow steady the ship. I'll allow you the reader to decide what that something was, I would love to know.

All I do know is that I have never felt alone, every step of the way. Whenever there have been difficult decisions that needed making, I have felt as though I could trust myself due to this stronger inner belief. There have been times when the charity has been under enormous stress, mostly from outside influences, however tempting it was to go into flight mode, I have had this greater resilience to ride it out and put incredibly challenging situations into perspective. Despite claiming not to be overly religious, more open-minded, I still find myself having constant internal dialogue during challenging times. I remember right at the beginning asking for direction 'just show me the way', whatever opportunity presented itself I saw as 'the way'. Interestingly as I look back, I can honestly say all those moments led to where I am today on my journey, even the ones that appear futile but added something to the ingredients that helped me get to the place I am in my life.

I'm 59 as I write this and today is a public holiday. I spent this morning at work carrying in 2400 meters of timber into storage, am I mad? I think not. I believe every business or charity that succeeds needs a strong engine to drive it, for many years I have been the engine in my own recovery, and Cornerstone the charity. Over the years, as our team has grown, the engine has become stronger, not because my engine has grown, but others have contributed to increasing the engine's capacity. This is our future, share and grow together. I'm closing in on the handover stage of the charity, I find it very difficult, but know that the engine is powerful enough to continue. You can have the most powerful engine in the world but without direction, it's pretty pointless, this is the area I find myself working on and encouraging confidence to steer on a daily basis.

I have had, and continue to have, so much pleasure looking at staff members journeys. Most come from not necessarily homelessness, but certainly a place of little confidence. To help nurture, support, and encourage has been a wonderful experience as they have grown not only as valued staff members but people. Watching them slowly get a sense of ownership within the charity has been truly liberating and something I hold dear to my heart. To watch them in stressful situations holding themselves admirably and seeing others look to them for support and encouragement as they once did with me is again wonderful.

Every single person, including all the clients that have walked through our doors, have unknowingly been part of the deal that I made all those years ago. They have made it so much easier for me to hold up my end of the deal, and for that I am eternally grateful.

In writing this little book of grief I have felt a strong sense of guilt. Guilt from knowing that while recounting my journey I am very aware that many others have not yet found their way. I still have the occasional vivid dream where I don't want to wake up because Cheryl has had a strong warm presence, or a trigger I may see on TV that drags me right back to that gut-wrenching hollow void within that can never be truly filled. When I look at my own growth, I remember being smothered and consumed in painful uncontrollable grief that would render me numb. Today, I can see things from a different, far less painful perspective. The feelings are still very real but more rational and controllable.

I have learned over the time since I lost Cheryl that the greatest gift you can give someone is choice. I suppose this is only ever evident when your choices are taken away. The choice to be happy or sad. I can look back at Ashley's relationship with her parents and see clearly that Ashley was given choices, the decision making was down to her. There's little doubt she knew what her parents and family wanted, but she had to make her own choices. I believe to this day that Ashley was only one positive relationship from turning her life around, all the ingredients were there for her to succeed. My personal view is that choice is what we trade with at Cornerstone, we give people choices. Whether the choices are appealing to them is a whole different debate, but if we can offer the faintest glimmer of light we would hope with our support it will go some way to illuminating the way.

Where is Cornerstone today? Well, we have come a long way since those lonely 10 years on my own. I no longer have to finance our efforts which I have to say is a relief. Today we have 40 emergency and supported beds spread across two counties. A factory manufacturing wooden furniture and sheds that creates employment and training opportunities. An alternative education provision that engages with children who struggle with mainstream education, or have disengaged. 95% of our adult clients reported experiencing the very issues our young people do during their education. This is why the provision was created to help young people succeed and hopefully break the likely cycle to low self esteem through under achieving in an unequal formal educational environment. We have two community hubs in two different towns that host various groups for those most marginalized in both communities. The Hubs are vibrant, and I enjoy visiting and joining in the various conversations. It never ceases to amaze me the hope that people can find in desperate situations.

We run the homelessness outreach which see's us doing street sweeps on an evening to find those rough sleeping and offer support. Last winter we opened our hub on an evening to offer an alternative to those rough sleeping during the cold weather. They could come to our Town centre hub and have a shower, warm food, and drink. Inevitably they would drop off to sleep and we would do our best to make them comfortable till morning. I have met so many damaged souls through this work, and I have nothing but admiration for our staff who show an unbelievable level of empathy to gain their shattered trust. How easy it could be for any of us to find ourselves thrust into homelessness. One wrong choice, one bad relationship or friendship, a series of events in relatively quick succession with little chance of respite, each event compounding the decline of your mental health till your resilience has deserted you and you find yourself homeless. Add to this having no support from family or friends, either because they lack the knowledge or care to intervene, or because you may have burned those bridges. These are the recurring themes to the stories that I hear daily. Substance misuse often plays a part in homelessness and rough sleeping. This is generally as a result of bad decision making, often coupled with peer pressure at some earlier point in our clients lives. An example would be the school age children who attend our alternative education provision. Most will freely admit to using Cannabis, convinced it won't lead to anything else. I hear the same story over and over again from the adults we support who are rough sleeping, describing the beginning of their journey into substance misuse. A more worrying factor is the amount of our children who choose cannabis over their prescribed Ritalin for ADHD, because 'cannabis works better' which is their perception, and it is clearly cooler to use in their peer group than Ritalin. So what we are talking about is self-medication, the same as a lot of our rough sleepers, its easier to take the drug than deal with the consequences of not using it.

Two of the most treasured things in my life are my twin Granddaughters Charlie and Beaux. They give me so much pleasure and allow me to reconnect with my inner child. They are four years old and were born on the 30th of August, which is also the anniversary of Cheryl's death. They are a blessing. Often when I look at them, I can't help but cast my mind back to the deal I did 24 years ago and wonder whether they are a gift. On the anniversary of Cheryl's death I still get that awkward gut feeling, it tends to last till the twins burst into the room with their unbridled enthusiasm for fun and learning, I feel truly blessed.

This is my journey, it's not the right journey it's simply the path I found myself on and the way I managed to navigate the immeasurable grief that comes from losing a child, or for that matter anything that has a significant impact on your life. I'm as happy as I can be with my outcome today, because I have nothing to compare it with. I have no idea where my journey goes from this point, my goal is to raise the bar for me and those around me. What I do know is that I feel like the driver of my destiny by somehow wrenching the steering wheel from despair, I believe that places me in a strong position to live my life out with a fair degree of happiness.

Epilogue

Today I can understand the principles of the grieving process on the piece of A4 paper handed to me in hospital by the kind nurse. At the time, amid all the emotional chaos it meant nothing other than a possible route out of the pain.

Do I have any advice? I suppose I do, but I'm also pretty sure it wont be what the sufferer may want to hear. Embrace the pain, as bizarre as that may sound it is part of the overall process. You must experience the pain to work through it. I was told to treat my flashbacks like a tape recording and simply switch them off. For me that didn't work, I had to go through each and every flash back. I would grimace in pain, but it wasn't until I could allow the flashbacks to run their course that the pain they generated and the frequency of the flash backs began to subside. The same could be said of all the stages of grief, I had to feel the different emotional pains to understand them and what they were underpinning. By smothering the pain out or turning away I felt as though the fire was still burning and could reignite at any time without warning.

Speak to someone. As well as the internal dialogue try and find someone with whom you can share your thoughts. This will help you make sense of where you are and in your grieving process and subsequent decision making. It will also help you tease out some of your deeper or darker thoughts. Remember at this point you are unwell, as with any injury you not only need support, you deserve it! I have worked with so many people grieving over all manner of issues that find themselves 'stuck'. They are stuck because they haven't had the support needed to help them through the quagmire of feelings and pain, they've had nobody to emotionally hold their hand through their darkest times when the simplest of decisions seem impossible.

What do you do if you are helping someone through the process? Listen, don't try to fix the problem or hurry the person through their process because the pain is too much for you, it is about them. Don't try and identify with a similar situation you may have experienced unless invited to tell your story by the person in grief. Walk the journey with them, if they fall help them slowly back to their feet. When a situation arises explore options they may want to consider, but it must be on their terms. You must remember you are stepping into a very dark place when you help someone in grief, and at the risk of repeating myself your task is to hold their hand and help illuminate some of those dark area's to make them more manageable. To this day I can think of every conversation, however brief that helped me through my grief. To every person that offered me meaningful support and a listening ear I am enormously grateful. If someone offers you the opportunity to be the person of support you ought to be immensely grateful and treat the opportunity and the individual with the respect that they deserve.

Part of my acceptance comes from viewing my relationship with Cheryl differently. I still have a relationship with Cheryl, it just isn't physical. How could I describe my relationship? I love my daughter and subconsciously seek her approval in lots of things that I do, I still find myself in situations and wish she was with me to experience the moment. My relationship allows her to be with me in my subconscious, I can imagine the pleasure she would have had, that in turn offers me some pleasure. When I'm in a situation where the charity receives recognition, I often feel emotional. This stems from the deal that I did and the knowledge that Cheryl's existence impacted hugely on the choices that I have made. It feels like she is alongside me, I get comfort from this and never allow myself to feel silly for having such thoughts. I deserve it! I'm a veteran of grief and a survivor, I deserve every positive from a tragically negative situation that comes my way, and so do you!

About the Author

Ernest Vasey is a 59 years charity CEO and psychotherapist from County Durham, England. He started his working life as a plumber from where he progressed to eventually having his own business. Steve was, and still is a fan of 1970's punk rock and ska music. He's a strong believer that the punk movement allowed so many young people from his generation to have a voice that empowered them and formed a lifelong belief system that leans toward supporting those most marginalized in society. Steve has a son Lee from his marriage to Cheryl's Mother Lynn, Partner Kate, two stepdaughters Nicky and Pip, and twin granddaughters Beaux and Charlie. If you would like to contact Steve, you can via

Email: ernest.s.vasey@gmail.com

or you can find him on social media

Facebook https://www.facebook.com/profile.php?id=100094057638164

Instagram https://www.instagram.com/ernest.s.vasey/

Twitter @ernestvasey

www.ingramcontent.com/pod-product-compliance
Lightning Source LLC
Chambersburg PA
CBHW061225070526
44584CB00029B/3992